MORAL DILEMMAS

GENETIC ENGINEERING

The
Manch
Coll
be a

Sally Morgan

Evans

EVANS BROTHERS LIMITED

First published in 1997 by Evans Brothers Limited

Evans Brothers Limited
2a Portman Mansions
Chiltern Street
London W1U 6NR

© Evans Brothers Limited 1997
Reprinted 1999, 2001

Editor: Su Swallow
Design: Neil Sayer
Picture research: Victoria Brooker

British Library Cataloguing in Publication Data

Morgan, Sally
  Genetic engineering, - (Moral dilemmas)
  1.Genetic engineering - Juvenile literature
  2.Genetic engineering - Moral and ethical aspects - Juvenile literature
  I.Title
  660.6'5

ISBN 0237517396

VISIT OUR WEBSITE
Evans
www.evansbooks.co.uk

ACKNOWLEDGEMENTS

For permission to reproduce copyright material, the author
and publishers gratefully acknowledge the following:

Cover (Maincentral image) KenEward/Science Photo Library (back cover) Will Deni Macintyre/Science Photo Library **page 6** CC Studio/Science Photo Library **page 8** Alfred Pasieka/Science Photo Library **page 9** (top) Jon Wilson/Science Photo Library (bottom) James King-Holmes/ICRF/Science Photo Library **page 10** (left) Robert Harding Picture Library (right) Adam Hart-Davis/Science Photo Library **page 11** Manfred Kage/Science Photo Library **page 12** Peter Menzel/Science Photo Library **page 14** J. Howard/Sylvia Cordaiy Photo Library page 15 Robert Harding Picture Library **page 16** Weiss/Jerrican/Science Photo Library **page 18** PA News Photo Library **page 20** (left) Liba Taylor/Robert Harding Picture Library (right) Ecoscene/Steve Newman **page 21** Ecoscene/Angela Hampton **page 22** Ecoscene/Kevin King page 23 Johnathan Smith/Sylvia Cordaiy Photo Library **page 25** Ecoscene/Mike Maidment **page 26** (left) Ecoscene/Norman Rout (right) Sidney Moulds/Science Photo Library **page 28** Klaus Gottfredsen **page 30** Charles and Sandra Hood/Bruce Coleman Limited **page 31** Rosenfeld Images Ltd/Science Photo Library **page 32** Ecoscene/Chinch Gryniewicz **page 34** Ecoscene/Andrew Brown **page 36** Ecoscene/Peter Hulme **page 37** Ecoscene/Chinch Gryniewicz **page 38** Rosenfeld Images Ltd/Science Photo Library **page 40** J. C. Revy/Science Photo Library **page 41** Chris Priest/Science Photo Library **page 42** (top) Alex Bariel/Science Photo Library (bottom) James King-Holmes/Science Photo Library **page 43** Peter Menzel/Science Photo Library **page 45** Mark Clarke/Science Photo Library **page 46** Ecoscene/Gryniewicz **page 47** Dr Gopal Murti/Science Photo Library **page 48** Geoff Tompkinson/Science Photo Library **page 50** Barros and Barros/Image Bank **page 52** Li Ken Ai/Image Bank **page 53** James Stevenson/Science Photo Library **page 57** Jeff Cadge/Image Bank **page 59** Alan Gould/A-Z Botanical Collection Ltd

CONTENTS

1. WHAT IS GENETIC ENGINEERING?

The stars of the film *Jurassic Park* were the dinosaurs. According to the story they had been recreated from DNA. The scientists had taken dinosaur blood from the bodies of biting insects that had been fossilised in amber. They had removed the dinosaur DNA, repaired it and inserted it into the unfertilised egg of a crocodile and, a few months later, hatched some genetically engineered dinosaurs. But can this really be done?

It all sounds believable but, in reality, this kind of sophisticated genetic engineering is not yet possible. Nevertheless, as you will see later, science can already allow us to do most of these things - so Jurassic Park may not be very long in coming!

The term genetic engineering has become familiar over the last few years, but what exactly does it mean?

Every organism, whether it is a microscopic bacterium, a whale, or a human being, carries within it a set of instructions that tell the organism which materials to make, how to grow and how to reproduce. The instructions are in the form of

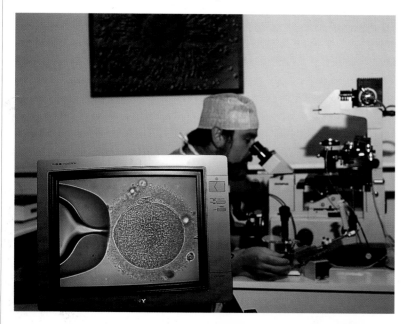

The egg is one of the body's largest cells and it is relatively easy to artificially fertilise it with sperm using a tiny probe. Now scientists can insert genetic information taken from another cell into the egg.

> *Am I really alone in feeling profoundly apprehensive about many of the early signals from this brave new world [of genetic engineering] and the confidence, bordering on arrogance, with which it is being promoted?*
>
> HRH The Prince of Wales

messages or codes and are stored in genes. These instructions are essential in the day-to-day running of the organism, and without the instructions life would not be possible. Genetic engineering is a deliberate change to an organism's genes. The result is an altered organism; one that has abilities or features that it didn't have before.

During the early 1970s, the first results of pioneering genetic engineering research were released. People in the USA were so worried that, between 1974 and 1976, all genetic engineering research was halted until guidelines were published to control the possible dangers. It was not until 1985 that the first genetically engineered organisms were released into the environment, in a type of pesticide.

Since then, genetic engineering has received a lot of publicity, both good and bad. According to some reports, for example, genetic engineering will allow us to produce 'designer' babies, even to prolong life indefinitely (see page 54). One thing, at least, is certain - we cannot ignore the issues, for genetically engineered foods and life-saving drugs are already in widespread use, and many more genetically engineered plant and animal species are being developed.

The latest developments in the field of genetics have enabled scientists to design and build life itself (see page 18). As a result, genetic engineering has raised many ethical and social problems which concern the environment, human health, animal welfare and agriculture. In many ways, our future will be shaped by genetic engineers. But how will society control them? Will they use or abuse their power? Genetic engineering is going to change our lives, but will it be for good or bad?

> *Our contribution to this debate [about genetic engineering research] is simple: we are all for it. We must not try to shackle the human yearning to find things out.*
>
> The Independent, February 1997

2. WHAT ARE GENES?

Your body needs a set of instructions in order to be able to function properly. These instructions are found in every cell, except red blood cells. They tell the cell what materials to make, how to grow, when to divide, how to repair itself - in fact, how to perform every process that goes on in the cell. The instructions are written down in the form of a code which is stored in the genetic material of the cell. This genetic material is inherited from your parents.

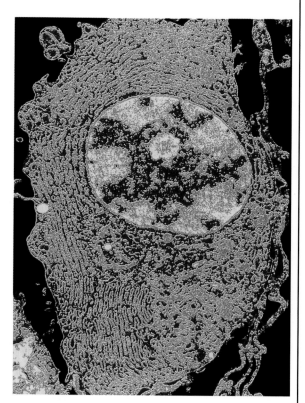

The DNA of a cell is found only in the nucleus.

Inside the cell

Your body is made up of millions of cells. In the middle of each cell is the nucleus - the control centre of the cell. It is here that genetic material, chromosomes, are found. A single chromosome is a very long, thin strand made of a substance called DNA.

A chromosome is sub-divided into genes. Within the human cell there are around 100,000 different genes, each with a specific job. So far, we only know the job of a few hundred genes but, within the very near future, scientists will know the position and role of every single one.

DNA is short for deoxyribonucleic acid. It is a huge, coiled molecule, so long that if the DNA from one cell was stretched out it would be one metre in length. If all the DNA in just one human were stretched out, it would reach to the sun and back fifty times!

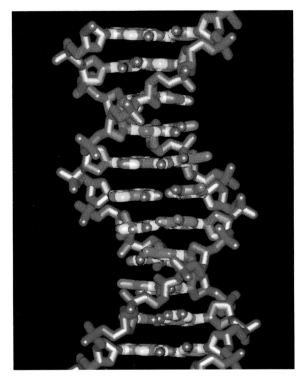

DNA is actually made of two strands twisted together in a spiral called a helix. It is rather like a twisted ladder.

Human Genome Project

One of the most ambitious biological projects ever undertaken started a few years ago. It is the human genome project, which aims to map all of the human DNA. The project will take fifteen years and will involve scientists from all around the world. By the time it is complete, we will know the position and genetic code for every gene in the human body. With this information, it will be possible to alter human DNA and carry out highly sophisticated genetic engineering on human beings.

What do genes do?

Much of our body is made of protein. Proteins are essential, as

Working in pairs

Most human cells contain forty-six chromosomes. Of your own chromosomes, twenty-three came from your mother and twenty-three came from your father, to make a total of forty-six, in twenty-three pairs.

The sex cells, eggs in the female and sperm in the male, have only twenty-three chromosomes each. When an egg and sperm fuse at fertilisation, the fused cell then has the normal number of forty-six.

they are one of our body's vital building blocks. One particularly important group of proteins are known as enzymes. These are biological catalysts, and they make chemical reactions in cells work faster.

Genes control protein manufacture in the cell, and tell it how to build proteins. A different gene controls the manufacture of each protein made by the body. If a gene is altered in some way, or damaged, the body will suffer from a malfunction. The disease cystic fibrosis, for example, is caused by a single faulty gene (see page 48).

Genes and your appearance

Your appearance tells us something about the genes that you carry. This is because your genetic make-up determines your appearance. For example, you may have dark skin because the gene you carry has the code for making the substance melanin, the pigment in skin.

In each of your cells, you have two genes for each characteristic; one given to you by your father, the other by your mother. Genes can exist in two forms, dominant and recessive. The gene for brown eyes is

Children inherit their genes from their parents. The new combination of genes produces a child who may resemble its parents, but has new characteristics as well. The colour of your eyes is determined by a gene inherited from each of your parents.

dominant, while the recessive gene is blue or grey. If you have brown eyes, at least one of your genes must be for brown eyes. The brown dominant gene will always mask the presence of the recessive gene. If you have blue or grey eyes, you definitely have two recessive genes.

Each new individual inherits all its genetic characteristics from its parents. The mixture of characteristics, and the fact that some dominant genes may mask recessive ones, produces variation, and makes us all different from one another. Although we are all human beings, and belong to the same species, there are enough small differences between us to recognise one another as different individuals. All species have this variation. Plants, for example, may differ in leaf length and petal colour.

Genetic engineering and forensic science

Your DNA is unique and, unless you have an identical twin, this means that no one else in the world has exactly the same genetic make-up. It was soon recognised by forensic scientists that this could provide a powerful method of determining people's identity and the genetic relationships between individuals. The techniques used to carry out these tests are often referred to as genetic fingerprinting.

If you compare the DNA between two individuals, you will find thousands of differences. Most of these differences tend to occur in the redundant DNA – that part of the DNA that the cell does not use. Even though

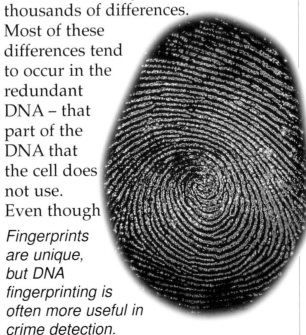

Fingerprints are unique, but DNA fingerprinting is often more useful in crime detection.

Identical twins

Identical twins are formed when a newly fertilised egg splits into two. These two cells contain exactly the same genetic information, so the twins will be genetically identical, and therefore will be physically identical. This is different from non-identical twins, which are formed when two eggs are fertilised at the same time. These twins will be no more alike than any brother or sister born separately.

it has no known function, it is passed on from generation to generation. Scientists estimate that there may be as many as thirty million differences between the genetic codes of two unrelated individuals.

How is it done?

The forensic scientist needs a cell sample in order to extract its DNA. Quite often, these samples are obtained from a crime scene. The scientists need only a very small sample, such as a single root of a hair, a tiny spot of blood, or a drop of semen. The DNA is extracted and enzymes are added to chop it up into millions of pieces of unequal length. This produces a unique set of fragments which are separated from each other using a technique called gel electrophoresis. This is a process in which the fragments are placed in a line on a sheet of gel. An electric current is applied to make the fragments move. The smaller fragments move further along the gel

The results of a DNA test are examined on a light box and compared with others.

than the larger fragments. Then the fragments are carefully transferred to a nylon membrane where they are fixed in position using ultraviolet light. The membrane is then treated with radioactive markers and X-rayed. The end result is a photo of a pattern of dark bands, forming a 'DNA fingerprint'.

It is important to remember that a DNA fingerprint does not identify every single gene. It provides a simplified profile, and it is very unlikely that two people could share the same fingerprint. In order to convict somebody of a crime, a judge has to be absolutely sure that the test is fair. So what are the chances of two people having the same DNA fingerprint? Scientists estimate that it is less than one in a million.

Genetic fingerprinting can also help immigration services to check whether someone applying to live in a country is in fact related to someone already living there and therefore eligible to take up residence.

> ### Catching the criminal
> In 1987, British legal history was made during a rape trial. This particular case was important because it was the first time that police had introduced a DNA fingerprint as evidence. When the accused man was shown the results of the genetic tests, he changed his plea to guilty, and was sentenced to imprisonment.

> **A DNA fingerprint is unique. Would it be acceptable for the police to hold a national DNA profile database to help them solve crimes? Should every adult be on the database?**

3. HOW DO WE ALTER DNA?

People have been altering the appearance of plants and animals for hundreds of years. Farmers have improved crop plants and animals by selecting those individuals that had the best yield to be parents to the next generation. But selective breeding is a slow and uncertain process. In the case of large animals such as a cow, the female cow may not be ready to breed for a year or two and she only produces one calf at a time. If the calf does not have the desired features, the process has to be repeated over and over again. It is also hard to predict the result, because a new combination of genes does not necessarily produce a better animal. For example, a cow that produces lots of milk does not always produce calves that give a lot of milk.

Creating new varieties

Some new types of crops have been produced by crossing two plant species. For example, oil seed rape only exists because two species of cabbage were crossed and a new species produced. This would probably never have occurred naturally, because the two parent

This newborn calf may have improved features, but it will be several years before it is ready to breed and pass its genes to a new generation of calves.

plants did not grow close together. Modern wheat is also a result of human intervention. Through selective breeding, modern wheat has three times as many chromosomes as the ancestral grass from which wheat was developed. The extra chromosomes have given modern wheat increased vigour and higher yields.

Genetic engineering is not that different to selective breeding. But it

Modern varieties of cereals produce higher yields than the ancestral grasses from which they have been bred.

Q

Is there any difference between producing a new type of crop by artificially crossing two plant species, or producing a plant with new features by genetic engineering?

is a rapid process and is far more precise. The genetic engineer takes a gene that codes for a particular feature from one organism, and inserts it into the DNA of another organism. The result is offspring that carry the new gene and have new features.

One step forward

The first problem facing the geneticists was to locate the gene they wanted. An even bigger problem was to remove it from the rest of the DNA. One of the most important advances in genetic engineering came when scientists discovered an

Q

Are we 'playing god' when we artificially alter an organism's genes?

enzyme that could cut DNA at a specific point. This meant that it was possible to take a piece of DNA from one organism and patch it into DNA from another organism. Geneticists now have thousands of enzymes available, each of which can cut DNA at a different place.

Inserting new DNA into bacteria has proved to be relatively easy, but it is not so easy to insert new genes into plants or mammals.

One way of getting the new DNA into a plant cell is to fire the DNA at the plant cells using an air gun! When DNA is mixed with microscopic particles of tungsten, it sticks to the surface of the particles. When the tungsten 'bullets' are fired at the plant cells, they pierce the cell wall, allowing the DNA to enter the cell and be taken up into the nucleus. And now there is an even simpler method. You take some plant cells, DNA, crystals of silicon carbide, and water and place them all in a test tube. Then shake well! The silicon carbide makes holes in the plant cell walls, allowing the DNA to enter.

Once the plant cell has taken up the new DNA, it is placed on a special growth medium. The cell divides many times to produce a mass of cells, called a callus. If treated properly, the callus becomes a new plant and all its cells will carry the new gene.

Making multiple copies

Once the DNA has been successfully incorporated into the cells of one plant, the modified plant has to be reproduced to make more plants. The geneticist has to make identical copies, or clones, of the original plant.

One way to get lots of new plants

A scientist examines a glass tube containing a genetically-engineered seedling growing in a liquid culture medium.

is to collect seed, but seeds are produced by sexual reproduction when the pollen of one flower fertilises the egg of another flower. The offspring would have characteristics from both their parents and, most importantly, the offspring may lose the new gene. So the plants must be multiplied using artificial methods of propagation.

Cloning is quite easy with plants. For many hundreds of years, gardeners have made exact copies of plants, simply by taking and growing cuttings. A section of stem is cut and placed in the ground. New roots and shoots quickly develop and it grows into a new plant, identical in every way with its parent.

Now, scientists can take just one plant cell and, using special growing media, produce an embryo plant. This is given a protective coating and then sown in the ground. Huge numbers of identical plants can be produced from just one original specimen.

Dolly the sheep

Dolly the sheep is the world's first cloned sheep. Cells were taken from a donor sheep and grown in the lab. Then an unfertilised egg was taken from another sheep and the nucleus removed. This made sure that there

The idea that you can bring back a child, that you can bring back your father, it is simply nonsensical. You can make a genetically identical copy, but you cannot get back the person you have lost.

Dr Wilmut of the Roslin Institute, Scotland, which developed Dolly

was no genetic material present. A nucleus was taken from a cell in the lab and inserted into the now empty egg cell. This egg was placed inside a surrogate mother sheep, where it developed as normal. Four months later Dolly was born. She is genetically identical to her mother. However she will never be totally identical because she will have been raised in a different environment and have different experiences. It will be a bit like identical twins. They may share the same genes but will have their own personalities.

Soon, the first human created from a piece of skin will be born. And the world will seem to shudder a little, and spin on.

Andrew Marr, The Independent February 1997

Q *Would it be right to clone a person? How might someone feel who discovered he/she had been 'born' by cloning?*

Dolly attracted a great deal of attention when she was first presented to the press.

When Dolly was two years old, scientists discovered that her chromosomes were suffering from more wear and tear than would be expected. Whenever a cell divides, the ends of the chromosomes get worn away and short chromosomes are a sign of ageing. Scientists are unsure of how this will affect Dolly and other clones produced in the same way. However, Dolly's daughter, Bonnie, has normal chromosomes.

In November 1998 the first cloned human embryo was produced using a cell from a man's leg and a cow's egg. Using a technique similar to that which produced Dolly, the egg's DNA was removed and replaced with the human DNA. This new cell was allowed to divide and grow into a ball of cells for 12 days before it was destroyed.

Research into cloning has continued. There are many rare breeds of animals at risk of dying out. Cells could be taken from these animals, frozen and stored for the future.

Q *Do you think it is right to add new genes to the DNA of an animal?*

GENETIC ENGINEERING

Transgenic animals

It is also now possible to insert extra genes into the DNA of an animal. The genes may come from another animal, a plant, or even a micro-organism such as a bacterium. An animal that carries foreign DNA in its own DNA is called a transgenic animal. The change in its DNA means that it is different from other animals of the same type - it is a new strain.

The animal that has received a new gene has new abilities. It may be able to make a new protein or enzyme, or produce a substance such as an antibiotic. The first experiments were carried out on mice. One of the first genetically altered mice had a gene which made it grow to a much larger size than normal.

There are now sheep with a gene taken from the angora goat, which produces a very high quality wool. Since angora goats are not easy to

keep, sheep carrying the angora's wool gene would make it easier to produce large quantities of angora wool.

Some animal genes can now be altered so that the animal can even produce a substance that would normally be difficult, or expensive, to manufacture. For example, a cloned goat produced in the USA carries a human gene. It produces milk which contains a substance which stops blood from clotting. The milk is collected and the substance extracted and purified. By altering DNA in this way, the goat has become a living 'drug factory'. (See also chapter 8.)

At the moment, the only way to produce new transgenic animals is to alter the DNA of normal embryos. This is an expensive procedure, so transgenic animals are very valuable. In the future, however, as genetic technology improves, scientists will be able to produce clones in greater numbers.

Is there a difference between altering an animal and altering bacteria?

Would you use a drug that had been produced by a transgenic animal?

4. FARMING FOR THE FUTURE

Today, there are 6 billion people on the planet. By the year 2030, the number will have risen to more than eight billion. The greatest increases are taking place in the developing nations, which are faced with a

Each year there are 90 million new mouths to feed. Farmland is in short supply so genetic engineering will help farmers produce more food from their fields.

major problem - how to feed all these extra people? There have been some amazing improvements in agriculture. The world's wheat harvest has increased four-fold over recent years, and the rice harvest has doubled. But, in order to achieve higher yields, even more fertilisers and pesticides have to be used. Not only are these agro-chemicals expensive to make and use, but they harm the environment.

Genetic engineering may help us to feed the world's people. In the future, we can expect farmers to grow crops that can protect themselves against pests and diseases. Crops will also be

Genetically engineered crops will produce larger harvests.

> *In order to find lasting solutions to world food problems, we need to work with sustainable agricultural processes which do not pose threats to the environment and human and animal health. Genetic engineering, like the so-called 'green revolution', is just another short-term dangerous attempt to provide a quick fix. It does not address the real problems of world famine.*
>
> *Greenpeace*

able to grow in more extreme climates, surviving frost and living in salty soils. For example, there is already a new potato in Peru which is resistant to bacterial diseases of the tropics and which can be picked within sixty days of planting, one third of the time taken by potatoes grown in Europe. There is also a new wheat, which can withstand drought and grow in acid soils. With these new crops, farmers will be able to grow food on land which was formerly unsuitable for farming.

Insecticides in plants

In Europe, our crops are eaten by a few pests, such as caterpillars and carrot flies. But, in the tropics, there are many more pests, some of which are incredibly damaging. Locusts, for example, devastate vast areas each year in Africa, consuming a whole crop in just a few hours. Even in a good year, African farmers often lose half their crops to pests or diseases.

One way to produce more food is to reduce the number of pests which eat the crops. The traditional method is to use insecticides - chemicals which kill insects. Many of these kill insects indiscriminately, destroying useful as well as harmful insects. For example, some insecticides will kill both greenfly and its natural predator, the ladybird. Others are specific and are designed to kill just one species of insect. However, apart from a few which are made from natural products, most insecticides

Spraying crops may be unnecessary when plants can produce their own pesticides.

are poisonous and are a threat to the health of people, especially the farmers who apply them. Many applications don't last long, and a heavy downpour can wash away the insecticide, forcing the farmer to use more. They are also expensive, and often not very effective. In the southern USA crops may be sprayed up to eight times a year, yet still one-sixth of the crop may be lost to pests.

In the future, farmers will use genetically engineered insecticides. One type makes use of a bacterium called *Bacillus thuringiensis*. This bacterium is found in the soil along with many other soil organisms. To defend itself, it produces a highly selective poison which has been found to be toxic to caterpillars, but harmless to other organisms. An insecticide can be made by growing the bacteria and then drying them to form a powder containing the poison. But the powder is difficult to use and not always effective. So, geneticists identified the gene that makes the poison, removed it from the bacterial DNA, and inserted it into the DNA of a tomato plant. The altered plant looked just like a normal tomato. To test it, the scientists took some normal and some altered plants and introduced some caterpillars. They found that normal leaves were eaten, but the leaves from the modified plant were avoided. The first stage of the experiment worked - the tomato had the self-protecting gene. But the scientists still had to answer a lot of questions. Were they sure that the

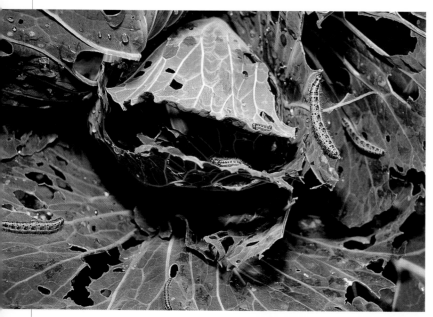

Chinese scientists have produced genetically engineered cabbages which produce a poison to kill caterpillars, especially those of the cabbage white butterfly.

Growing genetically engineered cotton may benefit the environment since it is resistant to the bollworm and does not require the use of pesticides.

'Bollgard'. The first crop was harvested in 1996 and clothes made from this cotton are on sale in the shops. The first Bollgard crops grew poorly and did not produce enough of the insecticide. Some farmers had to spray their crops to kill the bollworms. Since then the crops have improved. Record harvests have been reported and costs are down. Many farmers are growing Bollgard and now it makes up more than one quarter of the US cotton crop.

Some scientists are concerned about the new cotton, even though it now seems successful. The caterpillars are not actually killed by the toxin, just stopped from eating the leaves, so there is a chance that some of the caterpillars will learn to tolerate the toxin, and become resistant. There is more likelihood of this happening if these cotton plants are planted in increasing numbers across a wider area. Organic farmers are also upset, because they use the bacterial powder. Although it is difficult to use, they have no alternative method. If the caterpillars develop resistance to the toxin, organic farmers' crops will also be affected.

toxin made by the plant was exactly the same as that made by the bacteria? The poison must not be changed in any way, otherwise it might affect other organisms. Did it affect useful insects, such as honey bees?

Cotton is attacked by the bollworm. Now cotton plants have been given the self-protecting gene so that they can produce the toxin in their leaves. The new cotton is called

Sheep that shear themselves

Sheep need to be sheared at the beginning of summer every year. The hair of some older breeds of sheep

Q *Genetic engineering seems to be giving the sheep back an ability – to self-shear – that it has lost over time. Does this worry you?*

falls off naturally, but commercial sheep have lost this ability. Now, genetic engineers in Australia have managed to produce a protein that can cause the sheep to self-shear. They inject the sheep with a substance that temporarily stops their hair from growing at the hair follicle deep in the skin. After just one day, the hair starts growing again normally, but the halt in growth leaves a natural break in the hair. After four to six weeks, the break appears at the surface of the skin and the fleece can be peeled off the sheep. The only drawback is that the farmers have to wrap the sheep in a plastic 'hairnet' to stop the fleece dropping off before it is ready to be collected.

Fighting off the flies

Sheep are plagued by blowflies in summer. The flies lay their eggs in the sheep's fleece and when the maggots hatch, they burrow down into the skin and start eating. This leaves sores on the sheep which can get infected, and the sheep may even die. To prevent blowfly attack, farmers spray their sheep with insect repellent, which contains a number of different chemicals. It has to be applied several times during the summer. There is now a possibility that sheep will be given a gene which will enable them to secrete an insecticide from their skin, providing a natural year-round protection.

More milk

Cows produce a substance called bovine somatotrophin, or BST, which is a growth hormone. It is produced throughout the life of the cow, helping dairy cows to produce more milk and beef cattle to lay down more muscle. This hormone can be produced by genetic engineering. If dairy cows are given injections of BST every fourteen days they produce as much as twelve per cent more milk. In

Q *Which do you think is more harmful to the environment, spraying sheep with repellent or genetically altering the sheep?*

Cows treated with BST produce more milk but they are less fit.

some cases, milk production increased by twenty per cent. The cows digest their food more efficiently, so the dairy farmer gets more milk for less food and this makes his herd more profitable.

But BST is not good news for the cows. The cows tend to become sick more often. As a result, the cows have to be given antibiotics to keep them fit.

There is also concern that their milk can contain traces of BST. This means that the whole range of dairy products, from milk and cheese to yoghurts and baby foods may contain the hormone, as possibly also traces of the antibiotics. So far, scientists are unsure what effect, if any, consuming these dairy products could have on human health. BST is widely used in the USA, but has been banned in the European Union. It seems likely that this ban will be lifted in the near future.

> **Do you think it is right to induce cows to make more milk?**

5. DO WE WANT TO EAT GENETICALLY ENGINEERED FOOD?

Much of the food we eat already contains additives such as artificial colours, preservatives, and stabilisers. These additives are used to improve colour or flavour, or stop food going bad. Fruit and vegetables may have been sprayed with pesticides so that they are not spoilt by pests. There is now an increasing chance that our food also contains genetically engineered substances. Genetically engineered foods have already appeared in the shops amidst a lot of publicity, not all of it good. So, is there a difference between genetically engineered foods and so called 'normal foods'? And what are the benefits?

> **You say tomato, I say genetic nightmare.**
> *The Guardian February 1997*

The tomato story

Salad vegetables do not stay fresh very long. The foods spoil quickly on the shelves and cannot be sold, so there is a

Tomatoes (left) have a short shelf life and can quickly go mouldy (above). Genetically engineered tomatoes stay fresh for longer.

lot of wastage. If the ripening process could be slowed down, the producers would have more time to get their foods to market and there would be less waste. Tomato growers in the US have achieved just this by means of genetic engineering. One of the first genetically engineered tomatoes to be sold to the public in the US is marketed as the 'flavr saver' tomato. This tomato stays in top condition for several days longer than other tomatoes.

The perfect purée

Twenty years ago, scientists first started to study the ripening of the tomato. Their aim was not to produce a better tomato, but to develop a fruit that could be transported without refrigeration, while retaining its texture and flavour. They also wanted to produce high quality fruit juices and purées that required less processing and fewer additives. They identified an enzyme called pectinase, which helped ripening by breaking down the pectin which holds the plant cell walls together, allowing the fruit to soften.

By removing the gene, cutting a bit off, and then replacing the gene, they were able to stop the enzyme from working. The altered tomato ripened more slowly, remained firm, was easy to handle during transport, and there was much less waste. This new tomato is now being used in tomato purée. Purées cannot be too wet, and excess water has to be removed. The new tomatoes contain less water, so less energy is used during the processing, which means the genetically engineered purée is cheaper than conventional purée.

Trouble with soya beans

1996 saw the first harvest of a genetically altered soya bean. Soya is a remarkably useful product, and is found in sixty per cent of supermarket foods. It is high in protein and is a good binding agent, so it is ideal for use in processed foods such as pasta sauces, tinned soup, puddings, doughnuts, cakes, bread, biscuits, meat, baby food and diet foods, to name just a few. The US grows

Is there a difference between a tomato that has been improved by switching off one of its own genes and a tomato that has been altered by the addition of a gene from another organism?

nearly half of the world's annual total of 135 million metric tonnes of soya beans. It is the second largest American crop.

The genetically engineered soya bean has been designed so that it is unaffected by a weed killer containing glyphosate. This means that the farmer can spray the fields to get rid of weeds without affecting the crop, a big advantage. Before the arrival of this soya bean, farmers could only use selective weed-killers, which were expensive.

The company that developed the new soya bean, Monsanto, discovered a soil bacterium that was resistant to glyphosate, found the gene which was responsible, and inserted it into the bean. Interestingly, the same company which developed the soya bean is also the manufacturer of the glyphosate weed killer, so a farmer buying these seeds has to buy the weed killer from the same source. The seeds are more

> *The beans are the same beans. They are indistinguishable. You cannot tell them apart. There is no reason for the beans to be labelled.*
>
> Monsanto

A demonstration in December 1996 in Arhus harbour, Denmark, against the import of genetically engineered soya beans

expensive, but the weed killer is cheaper, and together they give better yields.

The amount of farmland planted with genetically engineered soya bean has increased to one in every seven hectares. Once harvested, the genetically engineered beans are mixed with the normal beans. Both beans look the same, so there is no way of telling them apart. Together, they go to the food processors and end up in our food. Many people around the world are very annoyed that we do not know that we are eating genetically engineered food, and do not have the option of choosing. They don't necessarily mind that the beans are being grown, but they do want to know if the foods they buy contain the beans so that they can decide for themselves whether

> *This soya bean poses an unacceptable risk to human health and the environment. The growing European opposition to the genetically engineered soya beans indicates that consumers do not want to be Monsanto's guinea pigs.*
>
> Greenpeace

or not to eat them. In the US, both soya bean farmers and the company that produces the plants are being challenged by an increasingly active campaign led by Greenpeace.

Supermarkets and food sellers are responding to their customers' demands for labelling. They are identifying GM soya in the list of ingredients on the label, and using the term 'GM-free' which means the food does not contain any genetically engineered or modified products.

People are eating more organic foods because they know that these foods cannot contain genetically engineered ingredients.

European consumers are putting the soya producers under pressure, forcing them to devise ways of separating and

---

Do you think foods should be labelled if their ingredients are genetically engineered?

Would the words 'genetically engineered' on a food stop you from eating it?

labelling the engineered soya. DNA tests, which detect small amounts of genetically engineered soya, can be used to check that the beans have been properly separated. However, separating the beans will be costly and this will push up the price of many foods.

Prize potatoes

A potato that is resistant to frost would be a big breakthrough. It would mean that potatoes could be grown more widely, and over a longer season. The traditional way of producing new, improved varieties of potatoes by crossing and selecting was not producing results. Then, genetic engineering discovered a way forward. The flounder, a type of flatfish, lives in icy cold waters and

has a gene which makes special antifreeze proteins to protect its cells and prevent them from freezing. Scientists have taken this gene and inserted it into the DNA of the potato. But this raises a number of issues. Now that the potato contains an animal gene, is it really a vegetable? Will vegetarians be prepared to eat it? If this modification proves successful, this type of potato will be grown throughout the world and used in a variety of products, including crisps and chips. This may mean that shops will need to label some crisps as non-vegetarian.

Quite soon, consumers may also be able to buy a quick-fry potato. It has been engineered to have a low water content, which means that it will take less time to cook chips and crisps.

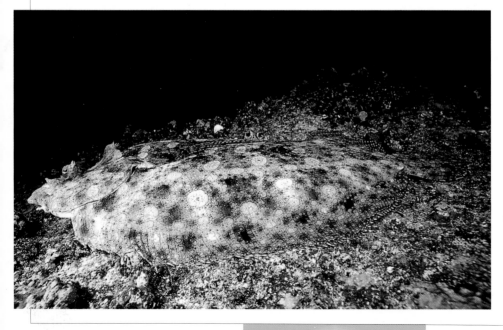

A gene from the flounder can protect potatoes against frost. But is this potato still a vegetable?

Making cheese

Cheese manufacture has used the same basic process for thousands of years. Milk is allowed to go off and become sour. It is then mixed with a substance called rennet, which causes the protein to clot and become solid. The solids, or curds, are separated from the fluid whey, pressed into shape, and allowed to mature. Rennet is a mixture of substances, including a protein called chymosin. Rennet is obtained from the stomach lining of young calves, so it is hardly surprising that vegetarians will not eat cheese made the traditional way. Genetic engineering has changed this situation. The gene to make chymosin was inserted in yeast and this engineered yeast now makes large quantities of pure chymosin at very low cost. Although the gene in the yeast originally came from an animal, cheeses made with the new chymosin have been approved by the vegetarian society in the UK. After some debate, they decided that they would approve the cheeses because they avoided the need to slaughter young animals. Cheeses containing the genetically engineered chymosin are clearly marked with the vegetarian symbol - the letter V. Nowadays, genetically engineered chymosin makes up more than half the world's supply of rennet.

Is it safe to eat?

Most countries have laws that require foods containing genetically engineered products to be extensively reviewed and tested. The products have to be approved by committees of experts to ensure that the product meets strict guidelines. The tomato purée now on sale in the UK has

Adding rennet to milk to make cheese. Most rennet is now produced by genetic engineering.

Maize is used in many processed foods. Should we allow scientists to insert a gene that could eventually make people resistant to a widely used antibiotic?

been through these procedures and was found to be perfectly safe to eat.

But there may be some quite surprising problems with some of the new products in the pipeline. One such is a new type of maize, which is an important food ingredient found in half the processed foods in the UK, including bread, cereals, dairy products, and animal feeds. Maize is attacked by a tiny

Q

Should consumers be told if animal genes have been added to non-meat foods?

pest called the corn borer mite, which chews through the stalks. A new type of genetically engineered maize has been developed to be resistant to the mite. But a marker gene was also added to the maize. Marker genes are used because they allow the geneticist to see if the genetic engineering has worked. Often, the marker gene is one that makes the organism resistant to the effects of a particular antibiotic. The marker gene in the new maize gives resistance to ampicillin, a widely used antibiotic. Scientists are worried that, when food containing this gene is eaten, the gene will come into contact with bacteria living in the human gut. There is a very small chance that the gene could pass from the food into the bacteria, making them resistant to the antibiotic. The companies producing the maize claim that there is no evidence that a gene could transfer in this way but, opponents say, there is always a first time. Furthermore, nobody is quite sure what will happen if we eat large amounts of foods which contain this gene. Some forward thinking companies have already decided that it would be wise to use other marker genes and avoid this problem.

Should genetically engineered foods be labelled?

Around the world consumers are demanding that genetically engineered foods should be clearly labelled. The question of whether consumers should have, or need to have, such foods clearly identified is a difficult one. Labelling could save lives. For example, some new foods contain a gene taken from nuts and anybody who suffers from a nut

In the past, biotechnology has fallen flat on its face. Eighty per cent of consumers don't want it. There is a big battle ahead and we are going to win.

Ronnie Cummins of the Pure Food Campaign in the USA

allergy has to be warned.

However, there is a difference between foods which contain the products of genetic engineering, and food that itself has been genetically engineered. For example, cheese containing an artificial rennet made by genetically engineered yeast, and tomato purées which consist of the modified tomatoes themselves. In 1992, the US Food and Drug Administration announced that genetically engineered foods did not need to be treated or labelled differently to natural foods. The European Union has ruled that products containing GM soya beans and genetically engineered organisms, such as tomato purées, must be labelled. Products containing genetically engineered ingredients which are chemically identical to the natural ingredient do not need labelling. However, many consumer groups around the world are calling for the labelling of all foods that contain any ingredients that have been produced by genetic engineering.

6. IS THERE ANY RISK TO THE ENVIRONMENT?

It is important to remember that genetically engineered organisms are living things, and so are much less predictable than artificial materials and chemicals. They can reproduce, move, and even mutate. Developments in genetic engineering take place in carefully controlled laboratory conditions. However, once a new or modified organism has been developed, it is likely to be grown outside. Once released into the environment, it cannot be recalled. In many cases, it is impossible to predict the results of contact with other organisms. For example, the organism could change or interbreed with others, creating new species. It is these risks that the geneticists have to assess.

It is vitally important that genetically engineered plants cause no more harm than the chemicals they are replacing. Some new crop

There is no way of stopping genetically engineered crops from breeding with wild plants.

strains contain genes that make them resistant to certain pests by making their own pesticides. This means that the farmer does not need to apply artificial pesticides, thereby helping the environment, saving money and conserving resources.

The unexpected

However, experience shows that the unexpected will happen from time to time, even with the best of safeguards, and serious accidents may occur. It has been found that genetic alteration of plants to resist viruses can stimulate the virus to mutate into a more virulent form, one that might even attack other plant species. What would happen if the genes for insect- and weed-killer resistance, introduced into crop plants, found their way into weeds? The result could be super-weeds which would be impossible to kill using traditional weed killers.

The genetically engineered soya beans (see page 27) have been studied in a few field tests. Nobody can be quite sure what will happen when the new bean is grown on a wide scale across the US. The greater the area over which the plant is grown, the greater the risk of something happening. There are many as yet unanswered questions about this plant. Here are just a few:

- will the new bean force out other plants?
- will it enter other ecosystems?
- will it genetically contaminate wild relatives or traditional strains?
- will it change in the long term due to its resistance to toxic substances?

Is there a threat to other animals and plants?

Some scientists think that genetically engineered plants and animals will threaten the survival of other species, and reduce diversity (the number of different plant and animal species). The genetically engineered plants may be more resistant to disease or pests, and hence they may grow stronger and be more successful than other plants. If they are successful, genetically engineered plants will soon be grown all round the world. The native soya bean comes from Australia and the Pacific islands. When the new modified soya bean is grown in these regions, there is a risk that the new genes will cross to the wild species. The wild population of the bean would be contaminated, which could affect local habitats and the species that grow there.

Oilseed rape cross-breeds easily with wild relatives. This may mean that genetically engineered oilseed rape would breed with related plants, and the new gene for resistance to weed killer could spread into the wild population. Some scientists predict that, within just one year, a large percentage of weeds growing near the crop would have acquired this gene.

In May 1999, the UK government announced that it was setting up an Agricultural and Environment Biotechnology Commission to look at issues connected with the release of genetically modified crops into the environment.

In the past, when people have introduced new animals to an

> *Are we going to allow the industrialisation of Life itself, redesigning the natural world for the sake of convenience and embarking on an Orwellian future? And, if we do, will there eventually be a price to pay?*
>
> HM Prince of Wales, Daily Mail, June 1, 1999

environment, such as the rabbit to Australia, the new arrivals have been too successful and have replaced the native species. So what will happen when modified salmon, trout, and carp are introduced to fish farms? These new strains of fish are twice as large and eat twice as much as their wild relatives. There is clearly a serious risk to the native fish if the modified species escape into the wild.

The fish raised on fish farms are enclosed by nets. Any damage to the nets would allow genetically modified fish to escape into the wild.

The terminator

Scientists are working on a method to make sure that any seeds produced by genetically engineered crops are unable to germinate. This has been nicknamed the 'terminator'. The crop plants will not be able to reproduce and the farmers will have to buy new seed each year. The terminator will also work if the crop plants manage to pollinate wild plants, so it will prevent the crops from cross breeding with wild plants.

'There's nothing to worry about.'
Do you agree?

Cleaning up the environment

Much has been made of the risks involved, and rightly so, but some genetically engineered bacteria could be extremely useful in our fight to clean up the planet. Over the years, a great deal of land around the world has been contaminated by toxic and radioactive wastes. Treating this land is not only difficult, but costly. Already, bacteria with natural abilities to digest certain chemicals are being used to clean up industrial sites. More may be done in the future, if we can design bacteria to break down the most poisonous of compounds and render them

Do you think using genetically engineered bacteria to clean up industrial waste is a good idea?

Cleaning up oil spills could in future be left to genetically engineered bacteria.

harmless. Research is already being carried out to improve the naturally occurring bacteria that can 'eat oil', for use following an oil spill. By applying the bacteria to oil-covered beaches, the complex oil molecules would be broken down into harmless sugars.

Saving on resources and energy

Industrial processes are very complex and, when making new chemicals, chemists make use of inorganic catalysts which speed up the rate of reaction. But these catalysts often need high temperatures, and acid or alkaline conditions, in order to work efficiently. In the future, genetically engineered organisms may be able to work effectively at lower temperatures, and require less extreme conditions. This will save money and resources, and will also produce fewer hazardous by-products.

For example, in paper-making, the wood pulp has to be treated with chemicals which break up the fibres and remove the lignin (the substance that makes up wood). The pulp is bleached so that the finished paper is white. This process produces a large volume of chemical waste that has to be treated before it is ready

for disposal. Genetic engineering may offer some help. Already, enzymes have been discovered in fungi which may be suitable for use as biological alternatives to some of

Paper-making produces large amounts of chemical waste which could be reduced by using genetically engineered enzymes.

the chemicals. Further into the future, it may be possible to engineer trees which have less lignin, and so require fewer chemicals and less energy to produce the pulp.

Plastic is made from oil. Its manufacture uses a lot of energy and produces a variety of polluting by-products. There is now hope that some forms of plastic will be made by living organisms. One biodegradable plastic, called Biopol (trade name), is made by bacteria. One way to make larger quantities of this plastic at lower cost might be to insert the gene into potatoes. This would save on energy, and reduce both cost and pollution. As our supply of fossil fuels (oil, gas and coal) dwindles, we may look to genetically engineered organisms to produce far more materials like plastics.

'Nothing to worry about'

The companies producing the new genetically engineered organisms do not think there is anything to worry about. They have a long and unblemished safety record of some twenty years and there is a rigorous regulatory system. There have now been hundreds of releases world-wide of genetically engineered plants and, so far, there is no evidence of any harm being done. The companies insist that they cannot afford anything to go wrong, simply because they face the prospect of crippling damages if they make a mistake and are sued.

Would you buy items made from genetically engineered plastic?

7. HOW CAN GENETIC ENGINEERING HELP MEDICINE?

We all need medical treatment at some point in our lives. Doctors can treat most diseases but there are some conditions that have proved difficult or expensive to treat. Genetic engineering is helping to overcome these problems.

Making vaccines

It takes a long time to manufacture vaccines. One method is to inject an

A long length of DNA taken from a virus often used in genetic engineering.

animal, such as a horse, with the weakened or dead bacteria that causes the disease. The animal's immune system produces defensive chemicals called antibodies. These are removed and used as a vaccine to protect humans.

Genetic engineering means that vaccines can be made quickly, cheaply, in large quantities, and without the need to use animals. The method is quite straightforward. DNA is removed from the bacterium that causes the disease, and the gene that carries the code for a protein is cut out and inserted into the DNA of yeast cells. The yeast cells produce the proteins which can then be used in the vaccine.

The way of getting the vaccine into the body may vary. One way may be to mix the DNA with a salt solution and then inject it into muscle, where it is absorbed by the cells. Alternatively, doctors may use a 'gene gun'. Microscopic gold beads, covered in the vaccine, are fired at the skin by the gun. The beads lodge just under the surface of the skin, and the vaccine is absorbed into the cells. Eventually, the skin cells wear away, taking with them all

Flu can be a life-threatening illness in older people. Every winter people can have a flu vaccination, but its protection only lasts a year so they must be vaccinated each year.

trace of the vaccine and the gold bead carriers. This means that the DNA would only be in the body for a short period of time, so the risk of affecting the body's own DNA is reduced. It also means that, depending on the disease involved, the vaccine may need to be repeated.

Tailor-made medicines

Flu is a very unpredictable disease. Every few years, a new strain of the virus appears, so people cannot develop an immunity to the illness.

There are some vaccines on the market, but they only work against one of the many forms of the virus, so they are only effective until the next new strain of the virus comes along. Since vaccines are expensive, it is impractical to produce vaccines against every strain of the virus.

But there is now much excitement about 'designer' vaccines. Scientists are trying to make vaccines from a single gene that makes a protein found in the flu virus. This vaccine may be able to protect against several different strains of the flu virus.

Doctors often treat cancers by giving the patient drugs that will kill the tumour cells. The treatment is known as chemotherapy. But chemotherapy drugs also harm healthy cells, so the treatment can cause a great deal of suffering in the patient. One way to make chemotherapy safer may be to give the patient new genes that will produce a chemical that protects healthy cells, but leave cancer cells unprotected.

It is not just drugs that will be made by genetic engineering. The gene for human haemoglobin has now been inserted into yeast. Haemoglobin is the oxygen-carrying red pigment found in blood cells.

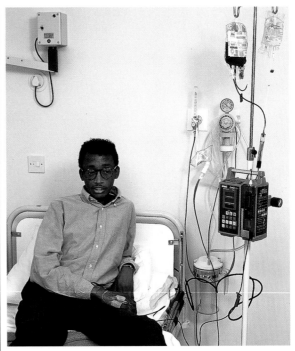

Hospitals need a constant supply of blood to treat patients.

Checking DNA fragments of chromosome 17, which has been found to be responsible for many cases of inherited breast cancer.

The yeast makes large quantities of this blood protein, which can then be used in artificial blood. In an emergency, it will be given to people who have lost a lot of blood.

Tracy the sheep

Genetic engineering has now made it possible for animals to be modified to make drugs for human use (see page 18). Some lung and liver diseases can be caused by a lack of the protein alpha-1-antitrypsin, or AAT. Patients can be treated by giving them the AAT that they lack. But AAT is very expensive to make.

Large quantities of blood are needed to make just a small amount, and patients need as much as 200g per year. But now there has been a genetic breakthrough. Copies of the human gene which carries the code for this protein were isolated, and transferred to a few sheep embryos. Four female sheep were born, each carrying the gene. These sheep produce the AAT in their milk. One sheep, called Tracy, produces 35g of AAT in every litre of her milk.

New organ donors

Every year, thousands of people die while they are waiting to receive a new heart or liver. The main problem is a severe shortage of donor organs, and this situation is unlikely to improve. The only way round the problem is either to find a source of artificial organs, or use animal organs.

The main problem with organ transplants is rejection. The patient's body recognises that the new organ is 'foreign', and so the immune system produces antibodies which attack the foreign organ and destroy it. Unless the patient is given drugs to suppress the immune system, the new organ will be rejected. Unfortunately, a side effect of the drugs is to reduce the patient's resistance to infection, so transplant patients catch diseases quite easily. They also have to take low doses of these drugs for the rest of their lives.

Scientists are now trying to engineer pigs so that, when a pig's heart is placed in a human body, there is no rejection. This is achieved by first altering the DNA of the pig

Genetically engineered pigs may be raised to provide a supply of organs for transplant operations.

making it a transgenic pig (see page 17). The transgenic pig grows organs which are covered in human proteins. When these organs are used in transplants, known as xenotransplantation, the human body is tricked into accepting the new organ, even though there are pig cells inside it. The first of these genetically engineered pigs have already been produced, and their organs have been transplanted into monkeys. However, experimental surgery involving humans has not yet been permitted.

It is not yet possible to make human clones (see page 18). But, in the not too distant future, this may become possible. The possibility would then exist for doctors to make clones which could be used as organ banks, bred to produce spare organs ready for transplant.

> *There is a need for transparency and openness in the activities of researchers and policy-makers involved in xenotransplantation, and for full debate about its acceptability.*
>
> Nuffield Council on Bioethics

Do you think it would be acceptable to breed human clones as transplant donors?

Is it right to produce pigs whose only role in life is to donate organs to humans?

Helping diabetics

When a healthy person eats sugary food, cells in the pancreas secrete insulin. The insulin keeps the blood sugar level steady, regardless of how much food is eaten. Diabetics cannot make enough insulin, so their sugar levels rise and fall steeply, causing many medical problems. Some diabetics have to inject themselves with insulin up to four times a day. Before the development of genetic engineering, insulin was obtained from the bodies of slaughtered cattle and pigs. Nowadays, it is made by genetic engineering.

First, the gene for insulin has to be located on a human chromosome and removed. This is done using a special 'cutting' enzyme. The enzyme makes two breaks in the

Young diabetics can inject themselves with genetically engineered human insulin.

DNA, one on either side of the insulin gene. It cuts the two strands of the DNA in such a way as to leave one strand of the DNA longer than the other. This creates strands with 'sticky' ends.

The second stage is called gene splicing and involves the use of a circular strand of DNA called a plasmid. The plasmid is broken open and the new DNA inserted. A second enzyme joins the sticky ends of the plasmid to those of the new DNA. The result is recombinant DNA - a DNA molecule made of DNA from more than one organism. This is placed in a bacterial cell, which now has both bacterial and

> **Q** *If you were a diabetic, which source of insulin would you prefer - that from a pig or from genetic engineering?*

human DNA. The bacterium continues to grow and divide as normal. But, it can also make human insulin. For commercial production, the bacteria are grown in huge quantities.

By placing the human gene into a bacterial cell, it is possible to make large amounts of insulin quickly. The bacteria are grown in huge vats and their product, insulin, can be removed easily. This method is very cheap and the product is very pure.

Using fish to cure diabetes

Fish are being turned into organ donors to cure childhood diabetes. If a child has a defective pancreas, he or she cannot produce insulin, which causes diabetes. One way to cure the illness would be to transplant healthy pancreatic cells into the patient's pancreas. But there would never be enough donors, and there would also be undesirable side-effects, so this is not a suitable way of treating children.

Tilapia fish grow quickly so could provide a regular supply of pancreatic cells.

The latest proposal to solve the problem is to use animal donors. The answer may be to use the tilapia fish. This tropical fish can be raised in small pools in large numbers. However, the problem is that the insulin the fish produces is not the same as human insulin. This is where genetic engineering comes in. The fish can be genetically altered to make human insulin. The human insulin gene is injected into the fish eggs, so that all the young fish carry the human gene. Their pancreatic cells can then be used in transplants.

Growth hormones

Many hormones, including human growth hormone, are now made by genetic engineering. Throughout our lives, tiny amounts of human growth hormone are released by the pituitary gland in the brain. It travels in the blood to muscles and bones, where it causes cells to divide and grow. A person who does not produce enough of this hormone is much shorter than normal, often less than 1.2m in height. Unfortunately, growth hormone taken from other animals does not work in humans. So the only way doctors could obtain hormone to treat their patients was by extracting it from the pituitary glands of dead people. Since each gland only contains a minute amount, this process was very time-consuming and extremely expensive.

It took 650 glands to produce just 2 or 3g of the hormone. At one time, human growth hormone was more expensive than gold of the same weight! Now it is made by genetic engineering and the cost of treatment has fallen dramatically.

Can we cure genetic diseases?

Many millions of people around the world suffer from genetic diseases. Genetic diseases are caused by defective genes, and as many as two out of every three people will die from a disorder that is caused, at least in part, by such a defective gene.

Genetic diseases include cystic

The gene that causes sickle cell anaemia causes some red blood cells to be sickle-shaped so they cannot carry as much oxygen as normal red blood cells.

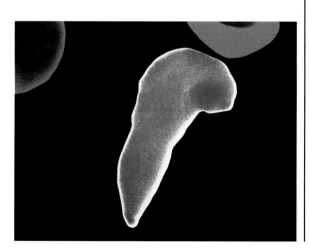

fibrosis, sickle cell anaemia, and phenylketonuria. The sufferers are born with the defects, which they have inherited from one of their parents. It doesn't take much damage to cause a genetic disease. For example, it is already known that over 3,000 diseases are caused by single-gene defects. The sufferer cannot do anything to cure the disease, since every cell of their body carries the disorder. All that doctors can do is to treat the symptoms. But genetic engineering may offer hope of more effective treatment to some of these people.

Gene therapy

Gene therapy offers hope to some sufferers of genetic disease. It is a method of treatment which involves taking diseased cells from the patient, altering their DNA, and putting them back into their cells.

The first successful gene therapy treatment took place on two girls suffering from the rare genetic disorder called ADA. Because of a faulty gene, their bodies were unable to make a critical enzyme called adenosine deaminase. The disease meant that their white blood cells could not fight disease, leaving their bodies wide open to infection. Until recently, these children would have survived only if they were kept in a germ-free bubble. The new treatment involved taking the human gene for ADA from healthy white blood cells of a donor and inserting the gene into the girls' white blood cells. These changed white blood cells were injected into the bone marrow, where they multiplied to form more white cells, spreading the healthy gene into more and more cells.

The best hope for gene therapy is on diseases which only affect certain parts of the body. ADA treatment was successful because it only involved treating cells in the bone marrow. It will be almost impossible to treat a disease that affects every cell of the body.

Treating cystic fibrosis

Cystic fibrosis is a genetic disease that affects the lungs. Sufferers have breathing problems and are prone to lung infections. They have poor digestion and produce abnormally salty sweat. The disease is caused by a defect in a single gene and it affects one in every 2,000 people in the UK. Fifty years ago, eighty per cent of babies with the disease would have died before their first birthday and, even now, few live into their twenties.

Is it right to alter people's DNA?

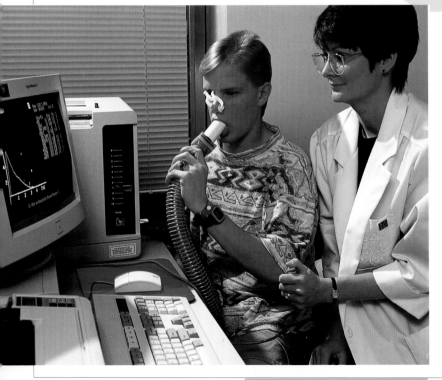

Sufferers of cystic fibrosis have damaged lungs so they cannot breathe in as much as a healthy person.

The faulty gene produces abnormally thick and sticky mucus which clogs up the lungs and blocks ducts into the gut, so enzymes can't reach the food. At the moment, the only form of treatment is to give intense physiotherapy. Patients are pummelled to make them cough up the mucus. They also have to take antibiotics, and drugs which relax the muscles in the lungs to make breathing easier.

In 1989, the gene for cystic fibrosis was located. At last, this meant that doctors could start researching a cure. One promising treatment involves the use of an inhaler, similar to those used by asthmatics. When the patient breathes in the spray, it is carried into their lungs where it is absorbed by the lung tissue. The spray contains genetically engineered viruses that invade the lung tissue. These viruses do not cause a disease, but act as a carrier to transfer a new gene into the lung cells. The new gene allows the cell to make normal mucus. Unfortunately, the cells have a limited life, so the treatment would have to be repeated throughout the patient's life.

8. BRAVE NEW WORLD?

Gene therapy has been dramatised in the media, and is often promoted as a miracle cure for all our ailments. But the reality is different. The treatment can only alter faulty genes. If there are no faulty genes, then gene therapy cannot help. It certainly won't change people's personality or IQ, yet it does hold out great promise for people who know they suffer from a genetic disease about which they can currently do nothing.

> *The idea that most of us are perfect is simply wrong.... On average everybody in Britain carries one or perhaps even two defective genes.*
>
> Steve Jones, Professor of Genetics at University College, London

Some breast cancers are caused by a faulty gene. This gene can be passed down the generations, from mother to daughter.

Genetic screening

As our knowledge of human DNA improves, it will become possible to check a person's DNA during a routine medical check-up. The genes for many diseases have already been identified, and their DNA sequences worked out. It is now quite routine in the genetics laboratory to check somebody's DNA to see whether or not a person carries a specific genetic disease. Doctors can even test cells taken from an embryo just a few hours old. This test is called genetic screening. People can be screened for genetic diseases such as

Q *Is it wise to screen somebody for a genetic disease when there is no treatment or cure?*

muscular dystrophy, cystic fibrosis, Huntingdon's Chorea, some breast cancers, Tay-Sachs disease and sickle cell anaemia. However, all this means at the moment is that we know if somebody has the disease. We still cannot cure them.

One reason that cystic fibrosis is so common is that parents do not know that they are carrying a gene for the disease. If only one parent has the gene, the children will be unaffected. But if both parents carry the gene, there is a one in four chance that their child will have cystic fibrosis. Because the gene has now been identified, genetic screening for cystic fibrosis is already possible. The parents give a blood sample and the DNA is extracted and examined.

Q *Would you want to know you had the gene for a genetic disorder?*

Doctors can then advise the parents of the risks to any child.

The pros and cons

There are both advantages and disadvantages in genetic screening. It will allow us to know whether we are likely in the future to develop certain genetic diseases. In years to come, we may even carry a genetic passport which identifies all the diseases to which we may be susceptible. As this becomes more widespread, companies may ask people to undergo genetic screening in the same way they currently have routine physical health checks. One danger is that people with faulty genes may be unable to get health insurance or jobs.

Some fear that people wishing to have a child or get married may be required to be tested to see if they have a clean bill of health. This is already happening in China, where the law requires that couples who wish to get married

The available evidence suggests that at present there is no demand for the genetic testing of employees, though the possibility of more widespread use in the future should not be ruled out.

The Nuffield Council on Bioethics

Q

Would you want your employer to know what genes you were carrying?

undergo screening for some genetic diseases, infectious diseases, and mental disorders. If one of the couple is found to have the wrong genes, they can only marry if they agree to sterilisation or long-term contraception.

These young Chinese schoolchildren will have to undergo genetic screening before they can marry or have children.

Are designer babies possible?

Imagine being able to design your own baby. Perhaps the doctor will give you a questionnaire about the characteristics you want your baby to have. You could choose its size, height, colour of hair and eyes, and perhaps even its intelligence. Then a computer will take

Q

Would you undergo screening before you got married?

> **In the future, it will be possible to alter somebody's genetic make-up so they did not have a disease – do you approve of this?**

the information and put it into a programme. You could then watch your 'baby' grow up. You could see what your child will look like at twenty, forty, or even eighty years old.

An unborn child can be tested for genetic defects.

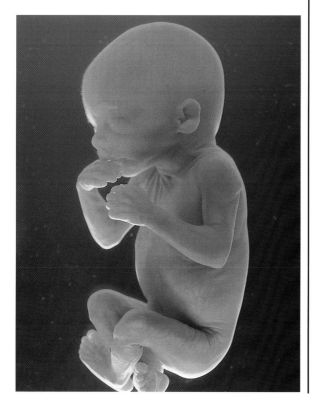

Does this sound a bit far-fetched? Well, it will certainly not be possible for quite some time. But by about 2005, scientists will know all the human DNA sequence, and will have identified the position, role, and genetic code for all the genes in the human body. If scientists can remove faulty genes and replace them with normal ones, then they could alter DNA to order to selectively change people's characteristics. Already, doctors can take a cell from an unborn child and test the DNA for some genetic diseases. If the child is carrying a defective gene, the parents can opt to abort the pregnancy. This raises the possibility that parents could terminate a pregnancy if they were not satisfied with the baby's genetic make-up.

Some features, however, may not be able to be genetically changed, simply because

> **People who decide that they want their Downs Syndrome baby may face the accusations that this is unfair on the unborn child and too costly for society as a whole.**
>
> *Professor Kaye Davies, Hammersmith Hospital, London*

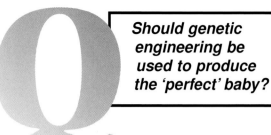

Should genetic engineering be used to produce the 'perfect' baby?

they are not controlled by genes. For example, scientists have not located a gene that controls one's personality. This is because personality is affected by the way a person grows up, their family, and surroundings.

Already, gene technology companies have developed techniques to genetically alter sperm cells in animals, so that certain traits are inherited in the offspring. Soon, it may be possible to do this to human sperm. This may be used initially to

> I don't see that nature has done such a good job that we can't improve on it.... I think it is rather primitive of us to be so fearful of ourselves.
>
> Novelist Fay Weldon, quoted in
> The Independent, February 1997

If doctors find an intelligence gene, would you be tempted to give your baby a higher intelligence?

eliminate unwanted genes, but who knows what will happen next?

Death genes

It is possible that the human genome project (see page 9) will reveal facts about certain genes that may be better left undiscovered. What if they found that certain genes determined how long we lived? This would mean that people could pay to have their 'death genes' removed, and live for ever. People could stay in prime condition, with cosmetic surgery to keep their looks. Perhaps there would be 'designer oldies' - older people who undergo a regular genetic clean-up to remove ageing genes. Although this seems unthinkable now, one thing is certain: if scientists do discover this, or similar, information, it will be impossible to stop people from using (or abusing) it.

Slimming the genetic way

Scientists working with mice have discovered that some mice have

Q *If the technology was available, would you want to live forever?*

defective genes which make them very fat. Some humans, too, were found to have this gene. The normal gene makes a protein called 'ob'. This protein is a hormone which affects appetite. When the gene is defective, it fails to make ob, the person's appetite is not controlled, and they eat too much. The result is a fat animal. So far, all the tests have been carried out on mice, but it won't be long before slimming aid companies start to think about the possibilities of gene therapy to solve this problem. By a simple gene repair, previously fat people would be able to control their appetites and lose weight.

Q *Would you take a special drug that ensured you stayed thin?*

9. WHO OWNS THE GENES?

If you buy a packet of seeds from a shop, you can grow them and, if you wish, you take cuttings or save the seeds to make more plants for next year. But this is not legal if you have bought a packet of genetically engineered seeds. You would not be able to reproduce the plant in any way because it is sold to you under a special licence that protects the seed producer's rights. The only way you would be allowed to get new plants would be to buy more seed.

Traditionally, farmers around the world save some of their harvest to use as next year's seed. In the UK, for instance, farmers may save as much as thirty per cent of their crop for use the following season. With genetically engineered seed, this is prevented under the terms of the licence.

But why would this be prevented? The reason is an economic one. The companies developing the genetically engineered plants and animals spend many millions of pounds developing the organisms, and don't want other people selling or propagating their plants and animals. They wish to legally own these new life forms, in order to protect their investments.

> *People are in this game to make money, and if they can't protect their discovery they won't bother to make discoveries at all.*
>
> Steve Jones, Professor of Genetics at University College, London.

Staking a claim

The issue of ownership of genes is a most important one, and lawyers all around the world are fighting the cases in court.

The companies staking their claims say that the finding, removal, and alteration of a gene is a scientific *invention*. Opponents believe that it is immoral to claim ownership over an organism's DNA. They claim that it is a *discovery*, which is quite different in law.

If it is a true scientific invention, then companies have the right to

Many of the decisions concerning the ownership of genetically engineered products will be decided in court.

protect it through the patent system. This system dates back hundreds of years. If you are an inventor and you produce something new and commercially valuable, you can protect your idea by getting a patent. This gives you exclusive rights to sell your invention for twenty years. A competitor cannot steal your idea and make money from it. In return, you must publish details of your idea. Everybody can read about your invention and see how it works, but they may not use it

> **We need comprehensive legislation. European laws are not good enough. There are ethical as well as environmental concerns. And it's dangerous that the whole of life is reduced to genes, that life can be valued as worthless or worthwhile depending on its genetic composition.**
>
> *Greenpeace*

without your permission.

Companies developing genetically engineered organisms want protection for their work, which is incredibly expensive, and they think the only way to get protection is to own a patent on the organism. As a result, they are busy trying to convince the courts that they are producing true scientific inventions, and not simply a discovery of something that was already there.

Already, one patent office has made an interesting ruling. A DNA sequence was discovered, a fact that would not itself have been patentable, but the company went on to invent a method of extracting and replicating the DNA, and the patent office ruled that a patent could be granted for the invention of the process.

Many groups of people disagree with this whole principle. They are very concerned about human DNA. They argue that, since the DNA is found in every one of us, the best way forward would be to make sure that all the information, including that

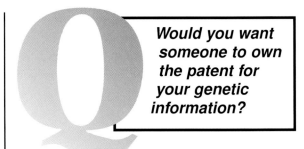

Would you want someone to own the patent for your genetic information?

discovered by the human genome project, is owned collectively by the people and not by individuals. Members of the European Parliament claim that human genes are the same as human life, and that patenting a gene is immoral, but the European Patent Office has disagreed and has decided that it is possible to patent human genes.

People are also worried that the major biotechnology companies carrying out genetic engineering will have too much power. These companies are in a race to discover and patent as many genes as possible. Once they have found a gene, extracted and patented it, other companies cannot work on the same gene unless they develop a different method. Each company will try to produce plants that can only be treated with a particular brand of weed killer, fertiliser, or pesticide, to lock in their customers.

But what about farmers in the developing world? Rich farmers of the industrialised countries may be able to afford to buy the new seeds

Do you think it right for a company to be able to own a particular gene?

each year, but it is very different for farmers from poorer countries. They usually save some of the harvested seed to grow the next year, purchasing only a little as a supplement. If they only have the option of purchasing genetically engineered seed, they will not be able to do this. Nor will they be able to afford the branded fertilisers and other chemicals needed for the healthy growth of the crop.

Over the next few years there will be some interesting court cases and decisions will be made that will affect everybody.

The story of the neem tree

The neem is a sacred tree in India. It grows everywhere and has extraordinary medicinal properties. For hundreds of years, people have made use of almost every part of the tree. Leaves of the neem stored with grain keep insects away, while leaf extracts are used to stop infections, keep mosquitoes away, and even as a contraceptive. Its twigs can be used as a toothbrush, because it stops tooth decay. But now companies in the developed world are using neem extracts in dental and skin care products and insecticides. They are applying for patents to protect their products and make money. People in India, who have known about the

neem for many years, seem to be in danger of losing out to commercial interests.

Who owns the rights to the neem tree? The people who have been using it for hundreds of years, or the rich companies who have only just discovered its potential?

GLOSSARY

antibiotic a drug that kills or inhibits the growth of harmful bacteria and fungi.

antibody proteins made by white blood cells to destroy disease-causing organisms which have invaded the body, and other foreign substances.

asthma a respiratory disease, sufferer experiences difficulty in breathing when exposed to certain substances or conditions.

bacterium a single-celled microorganism.

bone marrow the cavity found in larger bones where blood cells are made.

catalyst a substance which alters the rate of a reaction without being changed itself.

chemotherapy drug treatment given to cancer patients which kills the cancer cells.

chromosome a strand of DNA found in the cell, made up of many genes.

clone an individual that is identical with one or more other individuals.

cytoplasm all the contents of a cell except the nucleus.

DNA deoxyribonucleic acid – molecule containing genetic information

embryo a plant or animal as it develops from a fertilised egg.

enzyme a biological catalyst which increases the rate of reactions in living organisms.

fertilisation the joining together of a male and female sex cell to form a new individual.

gene a unit of inheritance, passed on from parent to offspring, made of a length of DNA.

hormone a chemical messenger, produced by special glands, which controls the various bodily activities.

immune system the natural defence system which protects the body against infection by disease-causing organisms.

molecule a group of atoms bonded together.

mutation a sudden change in genetic information from one generation to another.

organism any living animal or plant, including any bacterium or virus.

pesticide a chemical used to kill pests such as insects, fungi and weeds.

physiotherapy the treatment of disease or injury by exercise, manipulation and massage.

plasmid a circular length of DNA used in genetic engineering.
propagation artificial means of reproducing plants, for example by taking cuttings
protein a large molecule made from amino acids, important for growth and repair
sterilised made clean and free from microorganisms.
transgenic (of an animal) containing genes from another organism.

tumour an abnormal growth of cells.
vaccine an inoculation given to stimulate an immune response and to give immunity to a disease.
variation differences, a change from the normal.
virus a strand of DNA or RNA surrounded by protein which can only reproduce by invading a living cell.

INDEX